PEARL HARBOR

Copyright © ticktock Entertainment Ltd 2009
First published in Great Britain in 2009 by ticktock Media Ltd.,
The Old Sawmill, 103 Goods Station Road, Tunbridge Wells, Kent, TN1 2DP
ISBN 978 1 84696 897 6 pbk
Printed in China

CONTENTS

INTRODUCTION

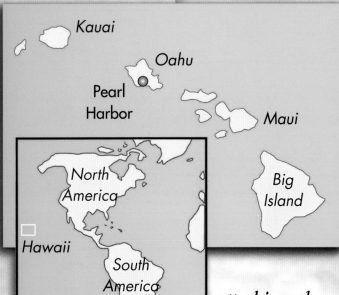

Kauai

Oahu

Pearl
Harbor

Maui

North
America

Big
Island

Hawaii

South
America

Above *This map shows the location of Pearl Harbor, on the Hawaiian island of Oahu in the Pacific Ocean.*

Below *On the morning of 7 December 1941, Japanese forces launched a surprise attack on the US Pacific Fleet, which was based at Pearl Harbor.*

On 7 December 1941 it was a sunny Sunday in Hawaii. Suddenly, early in the morning – while many people were still asleep or enjoying a peaceful breakfast – Japanese bombers launched a surprise attack on the US naval base at Pearl Harbor. In less than two hours, the attacking planes damaged or destroyed hundreds of US planes and more than 20 ships. More than 2,000 Americans – including civilians – were killed, and more than 1,000 were wounded. With this act, everything changed for both the United States and the world.

World War II had been going on in Europe since 1939, with the Axis nations of Germany and Italy fighting Britain, France and the other Allied countries. The United States was officially neutral in the war and at peace with all other nations, including Japan, which was part of the Axis. Americans were thus shocked and angry when a country that had not declared war on them launched an attack on US territory.

Before the attack on Pearl Harbor, many people in the United States thought that the country could stay neutral throughout World War II. The United States was still suffering from the effects of the Great Depression. Millions of Americans were still out of work. Many Americans thought that the United States should concentrate on its own problems rather than becoming involved in the affairs of other countries. Now, with an attack on US territory, war could not be avoided. The United States entered the war the day after Pearl Harbor was attacked.

The US Pacific Fleet had been moved from California to Pearl Harbor, on the island of Oahu, in 1940. At the time, Hawaii was officially a US Territory, located some 3,862 kilometres (2,400 miles) from the West Coast. Pearl Harbor is a natural, sheltered bay on the south side of Oahu. Ford Island, where the Pearl Harbor Naval Station was located, is in the centre of the harbour. In addition to the naval station, Ford Island had an airbase, oil or fuel storage tanks, and various buildings. Hickam Field, a large airbase, was found on Oahu to the south of the harbour. Japan hoped that by attacking Pearl Harbor, it could destroy the Pacific Fleet. Then the United States would not be able to stop Japan when it moved to take territory in the Pacific.

Before Japan attacked on the morning of 7 December all of the sites at Pearl Harbor were quiet. No one in Hawaii knew that a large fleet of Japanese ships and planes had taken up position a little more than 322 kilometres (200 miles) from Oahu. Beginning at 6 A.M., two waves of planes – 350 in all – took off from the Japanese aircraft carriers. Soon, they were flying over Pearl Harbor, dropping torpedoes and bombs on US battleships, destroyers, and other ships and on US planes. The attack took less than two hours, but its effects were devastating for the Pacific Fleet. In addition to the many planes and ships that were damaged or destroyed, 2,390 Americans were killed and 1,143 were hurt.

As a result of the attack, the world situation changed for the United States. On the mainland, before the attack was reported, it was just another Sunday. Three professional football games were going on. However the broadcast of the games was interrupted when the radio brought news of the attack. For the United States, the time for games was over.

Above After the attack, 'Remember Pearl Harbor' became a rallying cry for Americans as they pulled together to win the war.

Above Once American men began enlisting in the armed forces, women joined the workforce. Some took jobs in factories. The image of 'Rosie the Riveter' became a popular symbol of this new role for women.

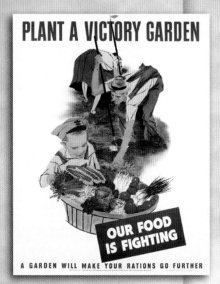

Above *During the war, women on the home front were urged to grow more of their families' food by planting 'victory gardens.'*

Below *A crowd of people gathered outside the White House in Washington, D.C., as news of the attack on Pearl Harbor spread across the nation.*

The day after the attack, 90 million Americans tuned in to listen to President Roosevelt's speech to Congress, during which he described the attack, calling 7 December "a date which will live in infamy." Roosevelt ended his speech by asking Congress to declare war on Japan. Within days of the attack, the United States had also declared war on Germany and Italy.

The United States became truly united in a desire to defend the country, win the war, and avenge the thousands who had died at Pearl Harbor. People could no longer ignore what was happening in Europe and the Pacific, because the war had been brought home to them. Japan had hoped that after Pearl Harbor, the United States would not be able to fight in the Pacific. Instead, the attack inspired Americans to fight, and millions joined the armed forces. Before Pearl Harbor, fewer than 1.7 million people were in the US military. By 1945, more than 7 million were enlisted.

Hundreds of thousands of Americans took jobs in factories producing ships, planes, weapons, and other goods needed to fight the war. With so many Americans back at work, the war helped stimulate the US economy out of the Depression.

The attack also had an unfortunate effect on Japanese-Americans. Many people in the United States were gripped with feelings of hatred for the Japanese, including Japanese-Americans, after the attack.

People were afraid that Japanese-Americans were loyal to the emperor, and not to the president and the United States. There were outbreaks of violence against Japanese-Americans, especially on the West Coast where many lived. In February 1942, President Roosevelt signed a measure ordering the relocation of Japanese-Americans from the West Coast. Some 120,000 people had to leave their homes, farms, and businesses to go to ten relocation camps, where conditions were harsh. They had to remain there until the camps were closed in 1944 and 1945. No evidence was ever found of any cases of spying or acts of sabotage committed by Japanese-Americans.

The world after World War II might also have been very different if Pearl Harbor had not been attacked. One of the biggest changes brought about by Pearl Harbor was the transformation of the role of the United States on the world stage. The United States was the only major power to come out of World War II stronger than it had been before. Americans learned new skills in the factories. They took a new interest in the world and its affairs.

Above *A poster for the film* Tora! Tora! Tora!, *released almost 30 years after the attack.*

Above *A poster advertising war bonds showed the leaders of the Axis nations: Italy's Benito Mussolini, Germany's Adolf Hitler, and Japan's Hirohito.*

CHAPTER 1

EARLY HISTORY AN EXPANDING JAPAN

Above *The Japanese felt threatened by Commodore Matthew C. Perry's armed warships when he sailed into what is now Tokyo Bay in 1853.*

Until the mid-1850s, the nation of Japan had no contact with other countries. Ships from other nations were not allowed to enter ports in Japan, and Japanese people were not allowed to leave the country or have contact with foreigners. In 1853, a US Navy officer named Matthew C. Perry arrived in Japan. Perry wanted to establish trade between Japan and the United States. Commodore Perry's arrival ended Japan's isolation. His visit put in motion events that would eventually result in the Japanese attack on Pearl Harbor.

"I have directed Commodore Perry to assure your imperial majesty that I entertain the kindest feelings toward your majesty's person and government, and that I have no other object in sending him to Japan but to propose to your imperial majesty that the United States and Japan should live in friendship and have commercial intercourse with each other . . . . These are the only objects for which I have sent Commodore Perry, with a powerful squadron, to pay a visit to your imperial majesty's renowned city . . . . friendship, commerce, a supply of coal and provisions, and protection for our shipwrecked people."

Letter from US President Millard Fillmore to the emperor of Japan, brought by Commodore Matthew C. Perry, 1853.

EMPERORS AND SHOGUNS

Japan was ruled by an emperor, a man that Japanese people believed was descended from the gods. The real power, however, lay with the shogun. The shogun was a military leader who governed in the name of the emperor.

Commodore Perry sailed into what is now Tokyo Bay on July 8, 1853. He came with four armed warships and 560 men. The Japanese felt

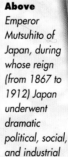

Above
Emperor Mutsuhito of Japan, during whose reign (from 1867 to 1912) Japan underwent dramatic political, social, and industrial changes.

"The United States of America and the Empire of Japan, desiring to establish firm, lasting, and sincere friendship between the two nations, have resolved to fix, in a manner clear and positive, by means of a treaty or general convention of peace and amity, the rules which shall in future be mutually observed in the intercourse of their respective countries . . . . There shall be a perfect, permanent, and universal peace, and a sincere and cordial amity between the United States of America on the one part, and the Empire of Japan on the other part, and between their people respectively, without exception of persons or places . . . ."

A portion of the 1854 Kanagawa Treaty between the United States and Japan, establishing trade between the two nations.

threatened by Perry's ships, which they thought looked like 'giant dragons puffing smoke'. Perry delivered a letter from US President Millard Fillmore asking Japan to open itself to trade with Western nations. The commodore then left Japan. When he returned in 1854 – this time with eight ships – he and the ruling shogun signed a trade agreement between the United States and Japan. In the following few years, Japan was exposed to Western culture and industry. The country went through great changes. In 1867, various groups banded together to overthrow the shogun and try to make the emperor more powerful. Although the emperor was supposed to be the supreme ruler, it was really the military that was in charge. Under the military, Japan developed a modern army and navy and new industries. Japan also developed new desires for increased territory and power.

Japan took part in a series of conflicts with other nations, gaining land with each war. Japan defeated China in the Sino-Japanese War in 1894–1895. This victory gave Japan control of a number of islands located to the east of China. Japan defeated Russia in the Russo-Japanese War in 1904–1905, a victory that brought more territory. It also brought attention from the West, since it showed that an Asian nation could defeat a powerful Western one. Japan annexed Korea in 1910. During World War I (1914–1918), Japan fought against Germany on the side of the Allies (including France, Britain, Russia, Italy, and the United States). At the end of the war, Japan gained control of land that had previously been under German rule in China and the Pacific Ocean.

It is our hope
That all the world's oceans
Be joined in peace,
So why do the winds and waves
Now rise up in angry rage?

"Universal Brotherhood," a poem by the Emperor Meiji (1852–1912) of Japan, who became emperor in 1867 and wrote approximately 100,000 poems during his lifetime.

TIMELINE
1853-1900

8 JULY 1853
Commodore Perry visits Japan.

31 MARCH 1854
Commodore Perry and Japanese officials sign the Treaty of Kanagawa.

1867
Japanese shogun is overthrown.

18 MARCH 1874
United States and Hawaii sign treaty giving the United States exclusive trading rights.

1887
United States gets full rights to the use of Pearl Harbor.

1893
Hawaiian queen is overthrown; independent republic is established.

7 JULY 1898
United States officially annexes Hawaii when President McKinley signs Newlands Resolution.

1894–1895
Sino-Japanese War is fought.

10 DECEMBER 1898
United States gets Philippines, Puerto Rico, and Guam from Spain at the end of Spanish-American War.

SEPTEMBER 6, 1899
United States declares an Open Door Policy in China.

FEBRUARY 22, 1900
Hawaii becomes a US Territory.

Above *A scene from the Sino-Japanese War, shown in a 19th-century Japanese woodblock print.*

 LETTER  **NEWSPAPER ARTICLE** **OFFICIAL SPEECH** ◎ **PLAQUE/INSCRIPTION** ◎ **TELEGRAM**

"We are a weak people, we Hawaiians, and have no power unless we stand together. The United States is just – a land of liberty. The people there are the friends – the great friends of the weak. Let us tell them – let us show them that as they love their country and would suffer much before giving it up, so do we love our country, our Hawaii, and pray that they do not take it from us . . . . We have nothing to conceal. We have right on our side. This land is ours – our Hawaii. Say, shall we lose our nationality? Shall we be annexed to the United States?"

Emma Nawahi, addressing a group of Hawaiians in 1897, to oppose US efforts to annex Hawaii.

THE UNITED STATES AND HAWAII

The United States also took part in a number of events that led to the creation of an overseas empire. Hawaii, a group of eight islands in the Pacific Ocean, had been an independent nation that was ruled by a royal family. In 1874 and 1875, the United States arranged trade treaties with the Hawaiian ruler with a specific interest in increasing trade. In 1887, the United States got full rights to the use of Pearl Harbor, on the island of Oahu. The Hawaiians called Pearl Harbor 'Wai Momi', which means 'waters of pearl', because the water contained many oysters, which produce pearls. The harbour provided a good place to repair and refuel US ships that were travelling farther into the Pacific. Hawaii has many natural resources, and the US wanted to control the trade in them. They helped overthrow the Hawaiian queen, setting up an independent republic in 1893. President William McKinley signed a bill – known as the Newlands Resolution – to annex Hawaii in 1898, and it became a US Territory in 1900.

A PACIFIC EMPIRE

In 1898, the United States defeated Spain in the Spanish–American War. As a result, the United States gained control of Puerto Rico, Guam, and the Philippines. Guam and the Philippines are located far away in the Pacific. Around the same time, the United States became active in China. Various nations had begun getting control of parts of China at the end of the 1800s. The United States wanted to share in the trade, so the country developed what was called the Open Door Policy. The United States reached an informal agreement with Britain,

Above *The US flag was raised at Iolani Palace in Honolulu during ceremonies to mark the US annexation of Hawaii in 1898.*

Right *Queen Lili'uokalani, the last monarch to rule Hawaii, was overthrown when an independent republic was set up in 1893.*

France, Germany, Russia, Italy, and Japan, guaranteeing equal trading rights with China for all of these countries.

JAPANESE EXPANSION

Japan was not pleased with the US presence in the Pacific. With its growing population, Japan wanted to have its own Pacific empire. This desire became even more important after 1929, when the world was gripped by the terrible economic downturn known as the Great Depression. Japan needed more territory to get the resources, food, and markets it wanted and needed. Under the emperor, Hirohito – who took the throne in late 1926 – Japan began taking steps to expand.

In 1931, Japan seized the Chinese province of Manchuria. The United States protested, but did little more. In 1937, Japan invaded eastern China. News of Japanese crimes against the Chinese soon spread around the world. The United States protested again and sent China some aid and arms, but did little else to stop Japan.

"She is a most formidable military power. Her people have peculiar fighting capacity. They are very proud, very warlike, very sensitive, and are influenced by . . . . a great self-confidence, both ferocious and conceited, due to their victory over the mighty empire of Russia . . . . Moreover, Japan's population is increasing rapidly and demands an outlet; and the Japanese laborers, small farmers, and petty traders would, if permitted, flock by the hundred thousand into the United States, Canada, and Australia."

Theodore Roosevelt, writing in 1909 to Senator Philander C. Knox, warning him about Japan; Knox was about to become Secretary of State in the administration of William Howard Taft.

Below *An injured child sits amid the rubble after Japanese planes bombed Shanghai, China, in 1937.*

"The killing of civilians was widespread. Foreigners who traveled widely through the city Wednesday found civilian dead on every street. Some of the victims were aged men, women and children . . . . Policemen and firemen were special objects of attack. Many victims were bayoneted and some of the wounds were barbarously cruel . . . . Nanking's streets were littered with dead. Sometimes bodies had to be moved before automobiles could pass."

Newspaper reporter F. Tillman Durdin, writing in the New York Times, 18 December 1937, about the Japanese invasion of Nanking, China.

TIMELINE
1904-1937

1904–1905
Russo-Japanese War is fought.

1910
Japan annexes Korea.

25 DECEMBER 1926
Hirohito becomes emperor of Japan.

29 OCTOBER 1929
US stock market collapses, beginning the Great Depression.

18 SEPTEMBER 1931
Japan invades Manchuria.

8 NOVEMBER 1932
Franklin D. Roosevelt is elected president of the United States.

7 JULY 1937
Japan invades China.

Above *Japanese troops march over the Great Wall of China during Japan's invasion of China in 1937.*

CHAPTER 2

BUILD UP THE EARLY DAYS OF WORLD WAR II

Before the attack on Pearl Harbor, World War II was mainly a European conflict. The United States did not want to become involved in the war and took steps to stay out. It became more and more difficult, however, for Americans to stand by while terrible things were happening across the world.

Above *Famed aviator Charles Lindbergh was a firm isolationist who believed that the United States should not become involved in the war in Europe or the affairs of other nations.*

Below *German troops march into France in 1940.*

WORLD WAR II BEGINS

In the 1930s, Adolf Hitler became the dictator of Germany, thus setting in motion the events that would culminate in World War II. It was to become a time that would throw all of Europe into chaos, and drag most of the planet into a conflict unlike any in human history.

Hitler had great plans to expand throughout Europe. He began by annexing Austria in 1938 and Czechoslovakia in 1939. Since Britain and France wanted to avoid war, they did not intervene. In August 1939, Germany and the Soviet Union signed an agreement that stated that the two countries would not attack each other. The agreement cleared the way for Germany to invade Poland on 1 September 1939 and this forced Britain and France to act. On 3 September they declared war on Germany – World War II had officially begun.

Germany quickly defeated Poland. After a number of months during which there was no fighting, Germany moved quickly in the spring of 1940 and invaded France, Belgium, the Netherlands, and other countries. By the end of May, Germany had defeated all except France. However, France could not hold out for long, so the

Above *Adolf Hitler, the dictator of Nazi Germany, attacked Poland in September 1939 – marking the beginning of World War II.*

MARCH 1938
Germany annexes Austria.

MARCH 1939
Germany annexes Czechoslovakia.

23 AUGUST 1939
Germany and Soviet Union sign non-aggression pact.

1 SEPTEMBER 1939
Germany invades Poland.

3 SEPTEMBER 1939
France and Britain declare war on Germany, beginning World War II.

5 SEPTEMBER 1939
United States declares neutrality in European war.

4 NOVEMBER 1939
United States passes new Neutrality Act, allowing sale of goods on 'cash and carry' basis

French government signed an armistice (a peace agreement) with Germany on 22 June. Britain was now the only free country left to fight the Axis.

US REACTION

In the mid-1930s, the US Congress passed a series of laws called the Neutrality Acts designed to keep the United States out of foreign problems. As World War II went on, however, people in the United States became very concerned. Most Americans were against Germany's actions, but many Americans were isolationists. They believed that government leaders should not make partnerships with other nations, and should avoid wars that did not involve their country's territory and self-defence. They did not want the United States to be drawn into what they saw as a European conflict.

Many Americans felt that their country had enough problems of its own. The United States was still suffering from the effects of the Depression, which caused widespread unemployment and homelessness. When Franklin D. Roosevelt became president in 1933, he had passed programmes that made people more hopeful and improved conditions. Many of these programmes created jobs in construction, industry, and even the arts that would put people back to work. Millions of Americans, however, were still out of work.

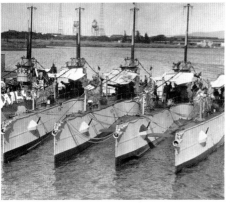

Above *The US Pacific Fleet was moved to Hawaii's Pearl Harbor in the middle of 1940.*

Above *Men sign up for the first peacetime military draft in US history, which was passed by Congress in 1940.*

President Roosevelt was an interventionist – a person who did not reject the idea of political or military involvement in the affairs of other countries when it was necessary. Roosevelt knew that Americans wanted to stay out of World War II. He realised, though, that the United States would probably have to become involved at some point. Although the United States was officially neutral in the war, the president slowly began to take steps against Germany. The US Congress passed a new Neutrality Act in November 1939. This act allowed all countries to buy US arms and other goods on a 'cash and carry' basis. This meant that the countries had to pay cash and transport the goods in their own ships. The act helped Britain and France who had large fleets of ships.

In the summer and autumn of 1940, Germany bombed Britain and made plans to invade. Roosevelt acted again, convincing Congress to strengthen the US military. In September 1940, he made an agreement to lend Britain 50 old destroyers that Britain badly needed. The same month, he got Congress to pass the first peacetime military draft in US history. In March 1941, Roosevelt got Congress to pass the Lend-Lease programme. Under this programme, the United States loaned Britain billions of dollars worth of ships, planes, and weapons that Britain could not pay for yet, but

"It is easy for you and for me to shrug our shoulders and to say that conflicts taking place thousands of miles from the continental United States . . . . do not seriously affect the Americas – and that all the United States has to do is to ignore them and go about its own business . . . . though we may desire detachment, we are forced to realize that every word that comes through the air, every ship that sails the sea, every battle that is fought, does affect the American future . . . . At this moment there is being prepared a proclamation of American neutrality . . . . And I trust that in the days to come our neutrality can be made a true neutrality, ... but I cannot ask that every American remain neutral in thought as well . . . . Even a neutral cannot be asked to close his mind or his conscience . . . . I hope the United States will keep out of this war . . . . And I give you assurance and reassurance that every effort of your Government will be directed toward that end."

Radio address by President Franklin D. Roosevelt to the American people at the start of World War II, 3 September 1939.

Right *President Franklin D. Roosevelt often used radio addresses to talk to the American people.*

Above *Emperor Hirohito of Japan (left in carriage) supported the efforts of his country in joining Italy and Germany during World War II.*

desperately needed to fight the war. Roosevelt also did something that attracted the attention of the Japanese. In May 1940, he transferred the headquarters of the US Navy's Pacific Fleet from California to Pearl Harbor in Hawaii. The Pacific Fleet, made up of battleships and aircraft carriers, was by then the only force capable of defeating Japan's powerful navy. Japan feared that the United States might use Pearl Harbor as a launching point for any future attacks on Japan.

JAPAN JOINS THE AXIS

In September 1940, Japan joined the Axis nations of Germany and Italy. Under their agreement, Germany and Italy approved Japan's goal of creating a Pacific empire. Japan was now able to take French territory in the Pacific, such as Indochina (now Vietnam), and continue its war against China. Many believed that Japan would soon move against the Philippines. In response, Roosevelt stopped the sale of certain US goods to Japan, including important resources like oil, steel, and iron. Japan saw these moves – as well as the transfer of the Pacific Fleet to Hawaii – as threats. Japan decided that to get the oil it needed, it had to takeover territory in the Pacific, including the Philippines. First, though, Japan had to defeat the US Pacific Fleet at Pearl Harbor.

TIMELINE 1940

MAY 1940
United States transfers headquarters of Navy's Pacific Fleet to Pearl Harbor.

AUGUST 1940
United States breaks Japanese Purple Code; learns of Japan's intention to refuse US demand that Japan pull out of Indochina and China.

2 SEPTEMBER 1940
United States makes destroyer deal with Britain.

14 SEPTEMBER 1940
United States passes first peacetime military draft.

27 SEPTEMBER 1940
Japan, Germany, and Italy sign pact which makes them allies in the war.

Below *German and Japanese officials toast the signing of the Tripartite Pact, under which Japan joined the Axis nations of Germany and Italy in 1940.*

We're in the Army now.
We're not behind a plow.
We'll never get rich while diggin' a ditch.
We're in the Army now.

We're in the Army now.
   We're in the Army now.
   We'll never get rich on the salary
   which we get in the Army now.

You're in the Army Now, *one of the earliest draft-related songs in the United States, performed by Abe Lyman and his Californians, 27 November 1940.*

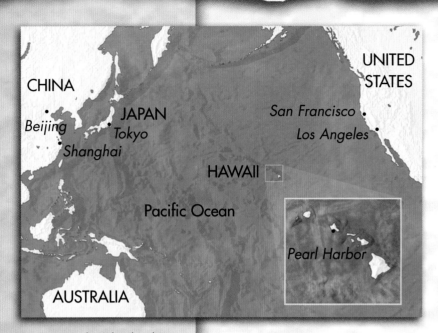

Above To reach Pearl Harbor, the Japanese attack force had to travel far across the Pacific Ocean from Japan to Hawaii.

Although the United States was officially neutral in World War II, to many in Japan – including Admiral Isoroku Yamamoto, the commander of the Japanese fleet – the United States was an enemy and a threat. In fact, Yamamoto thought that the US ships stationed at Pearl Harbor were like "a dagger being pointed at our throat". Under Yamamoto's direction, Japan began preparing for a daring attack on Pearl Harbor, hoping to strike a serious blow to both the US Pacific Fleet and American morale.

PREPARING TO ATTACK

In January 1941, Yamamoto began to develop his bold plan, which involved secretly moving aircraft carriers to locations near Hawaii and then launching bomber planes from the carriers. To help create the strategy, Yamamoto turned to Minoru Genda, a fighter pilot and staff officer. When Genda looked at Yamamoto's idea, he commented, "The plan is difficult but not impossible." The strategy that Yamamoto and Genda developed had a number of key points. The attack – which would use all types of bombing – had to be a total surprise. The US aircraft carriers were to be the primary targets. US planes on the carriers were to be completely destroyed. The Japanese ships would have to refuel at sea, and the attack would work best if it occurred during the daytime, especially early in the morning.

Beginning in April 1941, the Imperial Japanese Navy had a spy in Hawaii named Takeo Yoshikawa. Over the course of the next few

"The Americans were very foolish. As a diplomat I could move about the islands freely. I often rented small planes at John Rodgers Airport in Honolulu and flew around observing US installations. I never took notes or drew maps. I kept everything in my head . . . . My favorite viewing place was a lovely Japanese teahouse overlooking the harbor . . . . I knew what ships were in, how heavily they were loaded, who their officers were, and what supplies were on board. The trusting young officers who visited the teahouse told the girls there everything. Anything they didn't reveal I found out by giving rides to hitch-hiking American soldiers and pumping them for information."

🎙 **Takeo Yoshikawa, looking back at his activities as a Japanese spy in Hawaii in 1941.**

Right Admiral Isoroku Yamamoto, the commander of the Japanese fleet, planned the attack on Pearl Harbor.

Above *Japanese pilots and naval crewmen trained for months before the attack.*

months, Yoshikawa – who supposedly worked for Japanese diplomats in Hawaii – drove around the area and toured Oahu. He set up a telescope in an upstairs window of a teahouse on a mountain overlooking Pearl Harbor. He used the telescope to count the ships and planes located at the base.

Many in the Imperial Navy were against Yamamoto and Genda's plan, which was risky and dangerous. At one point, Yamamoto threatened to resign if the plan was not adopted. He received the support of the military, and preparations continued. Aircraft carriers were sent to the

"We trained fiercely, morning, noon, and night. We never had a day off, except when it rained. And we knew that we were about to start a war with America. We were shown drawings of ships on large cards and told to learn them. Two of them were the Pennsylvania and the Oklahoma."

Japanese pilot Yuji Akamatsu, who was among the men in the first wave of planes to attack Pearl Harbor, on the training leading up to the attack in 1941.

JANUARY 1941
Japan begins to develop plan to attack Pearl Harbor.

11 MARCH 1941
Roosevelt signs Lend-Lease Act.

APRIL 1941
Japanese spy, Takeo Yoshikowa begins working in Hawaii.

Above *Hideki Tojo, the Japanese prime minister, supported the attack on Pearl Harbor.*

JULY 1941
Japan invades French Indochina.

OCTOBER 1941
Hideki Tojo becomes Japanese prime minister.

NOVEMBER 1941
Japan and United States begin negotiations in Washington, D.C.

5 NOVEMBER 1941
Admiral Yamamoto sets 7 December as date for attack on Pearl Harbor.

Above The battleship USS Arizona sailed under New York City's Brooklyn Bridge when it was put into commission in 1916.

Japanese island of Kyushu, which had a bay that was similar to Pearl Harbor, so troops could train and practice there. Final approval for the plan was still needed from the emperor and the prime minister. In October 1941, Emperor Hirohito named General Hideki Tojo as Japan's new prime minister. Tojo was opposed to any question of pulling back from territory Japan had gained. He felt that this would hurt Japanese morale and cause a great loss of national pride. Tojo and Hirohito were both in favour of the plan to attack Pearl Harbor. With their approval, on 5 November Yamamoto set the date for the attack: 7 December.

For the attack to be a surprise, Japan needed to convince the United States that there was no chance of war between the two countries. Japanese diplomats thus began a round of negotiations with US diplomats in Washington, D.C., with the apparent goal of preventing war. The Japanese pretended to be considering US demands that Japan pull out of both China and Indochina.

On 26 November, while negotiations were taking place, Admiral Yamamoto ordered the Japanese attack fleet to set sail. The fleet consisted of six aircraft carriers (carrying more than 400 planes), nine destroyers, three submarines, two battleships, three cruisers, and seven oil tankers. The fleet was under the command of Admiral Chuichi Nagumo, a torpedo specialist with a great deal of experience sailing the seas. Minoru Genda was named to assist him as air operations officer. In the next days, the attack fleet crossed thousands of kilometres of open sea until it reached a spot some 354 kilometres (220 miles) from Oahu. The fleet, which refueled a number of times at sea, was not detected by the United States.

Japan's main target was to have been the aircraft carriers normally found at Pearl Harbor. On 6 December, however, Takeo Yoshikawa (the Japanese spy) reported that none of the carriers were at Pearl Harbor because they were

"By Imperial Order, the Chief of the Naval General Staff orders Yamamoto Commander-in-Chief of the Combined Fleets as follows:

1. Expecting to go to war with the United States, Britain and the Netherlands early in December for self-preservation and self-defense, the Empire has decided to complete war preparation.

2. The Commander-in-Chief of the Combined Fleet will carry out the necessary operational preparations.

3. Its details will be directed by the Chief of the Naval General Staff."

Navy Order No. 1, a message sent by the Japanese Naval General Staff, 5 November 1941.

Right Even as their government and military planned the attack on Pearl Harbor, Japanese diplomats Kichisaburo Nomura and Saburo Kurusu carried on negotiations with the United States in late 1941, pretending that they wanted to avoid war.

Above *Japanese dive bombers warm up before taking off from their aircraft carrier to bomb Pearl Harbor.*

TIMELINE
1941

26 NOVEMBER 1941
Japanese attack fleet leaves Japan for Hawaii.

27 NOVEMBER 1941
US officials send 'war warning' to all the heads of their Pacific bases, including Pearl Harbor.

out at sea. Genda was disappointed, and changed the main target to Battleship Row: the seven battleships moored along the southeast side of Ford Island. The large, powerful ships – the USS *Arizona, California, Maryland, Nevada, Oklahoma, Tennessee,* and *West Virginia* – represented most of the US naval power in the region. (Two battleships were not on Battleship Row. The USS *Pennsylvania* was undergoing work at Pearl Harbor's navy yard. The USS *Colorado* was being worked on at the naval shipyard in Puget Sound, Washington).

BREAKING THE CODE

The Japanese did not know that in 1940, a US military intelligence programme called Magic had succeeded in breaking the Japanese communications code – called the Purple Code – which was used to send messages to diplomats. Using Purple, the United States was able to decode and read many secret Japanese messages. The United States thus knew that during their negotiations, the Japanese were

Above *A Japanese naval officer gives instructions to bomber pilots before the attack on Pearl Harbor begins.*

"Although we hope to achieve surprise, everyone should be prepared for terrific American resistance . . . . Japan has faced many worthy opponents in her glorious history — Mongols, Chinese, Russians — but in this operation we will meet the strongest and most resourceful opponent of all . . . . Therefore you must take into careful consideration the possibility that the attack may not be a surprise after all. You may have to fight your way in to the target."

Admiral Isoroku Yamamoto at a meeting of officer pilots onboard the Japanese battleship Akagi, *17 November 1941.*

going to reject US demands that they pull out of China and Indochina. The Americans realised that this meant that Japan was probably going to declare war on the United States, and was planning a major attack. The question was where and when the attack would take place. To most US leaders, the likely target was the Philippines. The Philippines are located near Japan and would be valuable territory. If the target was not the Philippines, it would probably be somewhere else close to Japan. Few people thought that Japan would launch a strike against Pearl Harbor, located so far away.

On 27 November US military leaders sent a general 'war warning' to the heads of all US Pacific bases. These men included the military leaders at Pearl Harbor: Admiral Husband E. Kimmel, the naval commander of the Pacific Fleet, and Lieutenant General Walter Short, the army commander of ground forces. The leaders at Pearl Harbor were especially warned to watch out for possible sabotage of equipment and property. As a result, General Short ordered that the planes at Pearl Harbor be lined up together and arranged wingtip to wingtip, so they could be watched for signs of sabotage.

Above *Part of the machine used by the United States to decode secret messages sent in the Japanese Purple Code.*

DECODING THE LAST MESSAGE

On the night of 6 December the Japanese government began to send its diplomats in Washington a long, fourteen-part coded message, using Purple. The United States got hold of the message and began decoding it. The message indicated that Japan would soon reject US demands. When President Roosevelt was given the information that night, he turned to his adviser, Harry Hopkins, and said, "This means war."

"The representatives of the Government of the United States and of the Government of Japan have been carrying on during the past several months informal and exploratory conversations for the purpose of arriving at a settlement if possible of questions relating to the entire Pacific area based upon the principles of peace, law and order and fair dealing among nations. . . . It is believed that in our discussions some progress has been made . . . . Recently the Japanese Ambassador has stated that the Japanese Government is desirous of continuing the conversations directed toward a comprehensive and peaceful settlement of the Pacific area . . . . The Government of the United States most earnestly desires to contribute to the promotion and maintenance of peace and stability in the Pacific area, and to afford every opportunity for the continuance of discussion with the Japanese Government directed toward working out a broad-gauge program of peace throughout the Pacific area."

Telegram from the Japanese ambassador to the United States to the Japanese government in Tokyo, 14 November 1941, on US attitudes toward war in the Pacific.

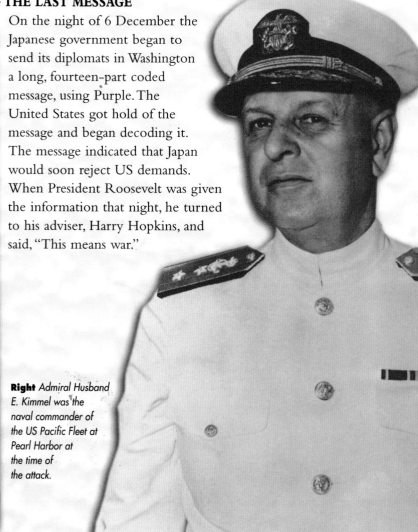

Right *Admiral Husband E. Kimmel was the naval commander of the US Pacific Fleet at Pearl Harbor at the time of the attack.*

Above *The USS* Ward's *number three gun and its crew were cited for firing the first shot in retaliation for Japan's raid on Hawaii. Little did they suspect what lay before them on the evening of 6 December 1941.*

THE WARNING COMES TOO LATE

The last part of the message, which arrived early on 7 December, told the Japanese diplomats to break off negotiations with the United States at 1:00 P.M. Washington time – which meant that war would be declared then. After this part of the message was decoded, it was given to Roosevelt and the commanders of the US Army and Navy. The US leaders now knew that a Japanese attack could take place at any time, but they still did not know where. Warnings were again sent to all US Pacific bases, including Pearl Harbor. There was a 5-hour time difference between the East Coast and Hawaii, so when it was 1:00 P.M. in Washington, it would be only 7:30 A.M. at Pearl Harbor. The warning to Kimmel and Short was sent to a telegraph office in Hawaii, where it arrived at 7:33 A.M. A young Japanese-American messenger got on his motorcycle to deliver the telegram to military headquarters. By the time he got there, it was too late. The attack had already taken place.

"This dispatch is to be considered a war warning. Negotiations with Japan looking toward stabilization of conditions in the Pacific have ceased and an aggressive move by Japan is expected within the next few days. The number and equipment of Japanese troops and the organization of naval task forces indicates an amphibious expedition against either the Philippines, Thai or Kra Peninsula or possibly Borneo. Execute an appropriate defensive deployment . . . . Inform district and Army authorities. A similar warning is being sent by War Department."

'War warning' sent by the chief of naval operations to Admiral Husband E. Kimmel, 27 November 1941; similar messages were sent to Lieutenant General Walter Short and other heads of US Pacific bases.

TIMELINE 1941

6 DECEMBER 1941
Japan begins sending fourteen-part coded message to its diplomats in Washington.

Below *A peaceful view of Pearl Harbor in October 1941.*

"Vessels moored in harbor – 9 battleships, 3 Class B cruisers, 3 sea-plane tenders, 17 destroyers: entering harbor are 4 class B cruisers, 3 destroyers. All aircraft carriers and heavy cruisers have departed harbor . . . . no indication of any change in US fleet or anything unusual."

Message sent from Admiral Isoroku Yamamoto to the Japanese attack fleet in Hawaii, 6 December 1941, describing the ships at Pearl Harbor.

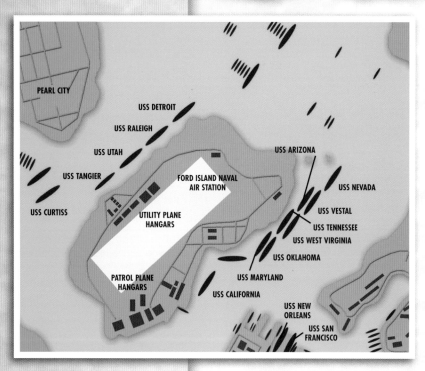

Above This map shows the location of the major US battleships at Pearl Harbor on the morning of the attack.

Map labels: PEARL CITY · USS DETROIT · USS RALEIGH · USS UTAH · USS TANGIER · USS CURTISS · FORD ISLAND NAVAL AIR STATION · UTILITY PLANE HANGARS · PATROL PLANE HANGARS · USS ARIZONA · USS NEVADA · USS VESTAL · USS TENNESSEE · USS WEST VIRGINIA · USS OKLAHOMA · USS MARYLAND · USS CALIFORNIA · USS NEW ORLEANS · USS SAN FRANCISCO

Below A Japanese Zero fighter plane, the main type of aircraft used by the Japanese at Pearl Harbor and during World War II.

The Japanese knew that Sunday morning was a good time to attack. On 7 December things were quiet at Pearl Harbor. Since it was Sunday, many sailors and soldiers were enjoying their breakfast or relaxing on the decks of their ships. The night before, the band from the battleship Arizona had won second place in a contest, so they were given permission to sleep late. The entire band – all between the ages of 18 and 21 – were killed in the attack.

THE ATTACK IS LAUNCHED

At about 5:30 A.M., the Japanese aircraft carriers were a little more than 322 kilometres (200 miles) north of Oahu, waiting for the signal to begin the attack. The Japanese turned their radios to the Honolulu stations, which were broadcasting music. No one at Pearl Harbor suspected anything unusual.

At approximately 6 A.M., the first wave of the attack began. Under the leadership of Commander Mitsuo Fuchida, 183 Japanese warplanes took off from the aircraft carrier *Akagi*. The planes, which included 40 bombers carrying torpedoes, would take almost two hours to arrive. As each plane took off, the men on the *Akagi* cheered. A second wave of 167 planes took off at 6:30 A.M.

At 6:45 A.M., the US destroyer *Ward* was on routine patrol near the entrance to Pearl Harbor. The crew noticed a strange movement in the water, which meant there was a submarine there. The *Ward* fired on and sank the vessel, which turned out to be a Japanese 'midget submarine' – a two-man sub carrying two torpedoes. Five midget subs had been released near the entrance to Pearl Harbor the night before. Lieutenant William Outerbridge, the *Ward's* commander, radioed a report to naval headquarters. Officials did not take his report seriously. They told him to keep investigating.

Soon, there was another warning. At 7:03 A.M., two privates – Joseph Lockard and George Elliott – on duty at a radar installation on the north coast of Oahu, noticed strange blips on the radar screen. These indicated a large group of planes was flying toward Oahu and was only 209 kilometres (130 miles) away. Lockard and Elliott telephoned the duty officer, Lieutenant Kermit Tyler. He told them that the blips were a group of American B-17 bombers on their way from California. Of course, Tyler was wrong.

> "It was like the sky was filled with fireflies. It was a beautiful scene – 183 aircraft in the dark sky. It was the most beautiful thing I had ever seen."
>
> *Japanese bomber pilot Abe Zenji, onboard the aircraft carrier Akagi, as the first wave of planes took off.*

THE ASSAULT BEGINS

At 7:49 A.M., Commander Fuchida ordered his bombers to begin the assault by radioing, "To! To! To!" Suddenly, planes were roaring through the sky, dropping their bombs. Fuchida then radioed, "Tora! Tora! Tora!" – which meant that the Japanese had succeeded in surprising the enemy. The attack was definitely a surprise. Bombs struck the airfields at Kaneohe, Hickam, and other sites. Torpedo planes began to attack the battleships, destroyers, cruisers, and other ships. Within just a few minutes, the battleships *California*, *West Virginia*, and *Oklahoma* were sinking. Many sailors were trapped below deck in the sinking ships; 429 men died on the *Oklahoma* alone. The *Utah* (an old battleship being used for training) capsized, with 58 men on board. Smaller ships were blown apart.

Above *Five midget submarines like this one, each carrying two torpedoes, were released near the entrance to Pearl Harbor.*

6:00 A.M.
First wave of Japanese planes take off.

6:30 A.M.
Second wave of Japanese planes take off.

6:45 A.M.
Destroyer *Ward* sinks Japanese midget submarine.

7:03 A.M.
Radar indicates large group of planes heading toward Oahu.

7:49 A.M.
Commander Fuchida signals attack to begin ("To! To! To!").

7:53 A.M.
Fuchida signals that attack was a surprise ("Tora! Tora! Tora!").

8.00 A.M.
Radio message sent out to ships and bases telling of attack.

8:03 A.M.
Battleship *Nevada* torpedoed.

8:04 A.M.
Honolulu radio station tells service personnel to report to duty.

8:05 A.M.
Battleship *California* torpedoed; battleship *Oklahoma* capsizes after being torpedoed.

8:10 A.M.
Bomb hits ammunition stockpile onboard battleship *Arizona*, which explodes.

Above Hit by a bomb, the battleship Arizona *exploded and sank within nine minutes, killing 1,177 men on board.*

The air was filled with smoke, and the water filled with oil spilling from the damaged ships. The oil caught fire, so that the sea was covered with walls of flame, burning sailors who had jumped out of the sinking ships. The most devastating blow was to the battleship *Arizona*. At 8:10 A.M., a bomb sliced through the deck of the ship, setting off ammunition on board. The *Arizona* exploded. Samuel Fuqua, the first lieutenant, became the senior commanding officer. He bravely directed the crew to fight the fires and help the wounded before he was forced to leave the ship. The mighty *Arizona* sank in nine minutes, killing 1,177 crewmen.

By 8:35 A.M., the first wave of Japanese planes ended their attack. Twenty minutes later, the second wave arrived. They continued to hit the Kaneohe and Hickam airbases and pounded the ships that had not yet been destroyed. Although the battleship *Nevada* was badly damaged, it tried to leave the harbour so it could put up a better fight. Sailors on other ships cheered as the *Nevada* managed to get under way, but the Japanese continued to attack. They hit the *Nevada* again and again. The crew feared that if they sank they would block the harbour entrance. This would have created great difficulties for the Americans. To prevent this, the ship grounded itself shortly after 9 A.M. Just before 10 A.M., the last Japanese planes flew back to their carriers. The attack was over.

"Well, I was out on deck doing the morning chores, which you did every morning . . . . All of a sudden, this plane come along, and [I] didn't pay much attention to it, because planes were landing at Ford Island all the time. And all of a sudden, the chips started flying all around me and the plane — it was strafing me . . . . I . . . . started back to my battle station and a bomb went off. I learned later it was back about turret number 4 — about where I'd been working about ten, fifteen minutes before. And evidently it knocked me out, ruptured both my lungs . . . . And all the lights went out . . . . I don't know how long I laid there . . . .

[There] was no panic down there or anything. But there was smoke and water knee deep . . . . and the senior division officer . . . . told us to all come out on deck and help . . . . fighting fire and so forth . . . . but there was nothing we could do. The ship was a total loss and the commander . . . . said well we just as well abandon ship."

🎤 **Carl Carson, who was onboard the battleship Arizona during the attack.**

Above Rescuers approached the battleship West Virginia, *which was burning and sinking after being bombed.*

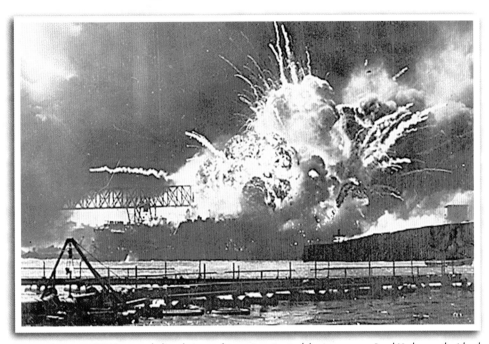

Above *Destroyer USS* Shaw *exploding during early morning air attack by Japanese on Pearl Harbor on the island of Oahu, near Honolulu.*

THE US RESPONSE

At first, many Americans thought the attack was some kind of drill. Lieutenant Commander Logan Ramsey, on Ford Island, thought so until he saw a low-flying plane drop a bomb just before 8 A.M. He immediately sent out a radio message to all ships and bases: "AIR RAID ON PEARL HARBOR. THIS IS NO DRILL." At 8:04 A.M., a Honolulu radio station interrupted its programme to state: "All Army, Navy, and Marine personnel to report to duty."

The Americans quickly realised that the attackers were Japanese. They could tell from the red circles – the symbol of the rising sun – painted on the planes' tails and wingtips. Some of the planes flew so low that the Americans could see the pilots' faces. Sailors, soldiers, and airmen rushed to their battle stations. They manned guns and began to fight back. Since the US planes were arranged wingtip to wingtip, they were not ready to fly. Fourteen pilots managed to get their planes in the air, however, and they shot down 11 Japanese planes.

> "I saw a torpedo drop and our guns were firing before they'd even sounded general quarters. I ran to my battle station and went through the rest of that day without getting fully dressed . . . . We could clearly see the Arizona and all of Battleship Row from our post. At one point we were all just standing there with tears in our eyes watching the devastation and feeling helpless, with nothing to be done about it."

Crewman Bill Speer, who had just stepped out of the shower on the light cruiser Honolulu *when the attack began.*

TIMELINE 1941

8:35 A.M.
First wave attack ends; Roosevelt tells Secretary of State about attack.

8:55 A.M.
Second wave attack begins; battleship *Nevada* gets under way.

9:00 A.M.
Crew of *Arizona* abandons ship.

9:10 A.M.
Nevada runs aground.

9:25 A.M.
Cruisers *Honolulu*, *St. Louis*, *San Francisco*, and *New Orleans* bombed.

9:45 A.M.
Attack ends.

11:00 A.M.
Fuchida flies over Pearl Harbor to see damage.

8 DECEMBER 1941
United States declares war on Japan; Japan invades Philippines.

9 DECEMBER 1941
Thirty-two crew members found alive on *Oklahoma*.

11 DECEMBER 1941
Germany and Italy declare war on United States; United States declares war on them.

DECEMBER 1941
Song 'Remember Pearl Harbor' released.

"above and beyond the call of duty"

DORIE MILLER
Received the Navy Cross at Pearl Harbor, May 27, 1942

Above A poster produced in 1943 of Dorie Miller wearing his Navy Cross (below).

"You understood exactly who they were, right away. I mean, you seen the Japanese rising sun on [the planes]. I just started immediately for my battle station . . . . They had a job to do, ... just like what we had to do, but the simple thing is that when you get in a ring with a boxer or a fighter, you know who you're going against. But when a sneak attack like that, it's something you have to think about, really think about."

 Seaman First Class John Martini, who was onboard the battleship Arizona.

Doris (Dorie) Miller was one of the brave sailors who responded to the challenge that day. Miller, an African American, was a cook's assistant on the *West Virginia.* After the ship was torpedoed, he manned a machine gun even though he had not been trained to use it. Miller became the first African American to receive the Navy Cross. Soldiers and sailors at Pearl Harbor received many commendations for their bravery that day, including 15 Medals of Honor, 51 Navy Crosses, and 69 Silver Stars. Although the Americans showed great heroism, there was also great confusion. They shot at 12 American B-17s arriving from California and 14 scout bombers from the aircraft carrier *Enterprise.* Some of the planes were shot down.

"It wasn't hard. I just pulled the trigger and she worked fine. I had watched the others with these guns. I guess I fired for about fifteen minutes. I think I got one of those Jap planes. They were diving pretty close to us."

Doris (Dorie) Miller on how he was able to man a machine gun on the West Virginia *in the middle of the attack.*

ASSESSING THE DAMAGE

At 11 A.M., Fuchida flew over Pearl Harbor to see the damage, which was considerable. Pearl Harbor was the worst naval disaster in US history. Twenty-one US ships were sunk or damaged, including eight battleships; 164 planes were destroyed and 159 damaged.

Right Admiral Chester Nimitz awards Dorie Miller the Navy Cross for his heroism aboard the West Virginia.

FEBRUARY 1942
Roosevelt orders internment of Japanese-Americans from West Coast.

23 JANUARY 1942
Roberts Commission releases report on Pearl Harbor.

FEBRUARY 1942
Censored newsreel released showing attack on Pearl Harbor.

Above *American servicemen salvaging what they can from wreckage of US warships damaged or sunk following Japanese surprise attack on Pearl Harbor.*

The Japanese lost only 29 planes and five midget submarines. The loss of life was huge: 2,341 US sailors, soldiers, and airmen were killed, and 1,143 were hurt. Forty-nine civilians were killed and 35 injured. The Japanese lost 64 men.

SAVING AND SALVAGING

After the attack, everyone who was able joined in the efforts to rescue and treat the wounded. Sailors were trapped in some of the ships that had sunk. Rescuers used drills to cut through the steel walls to reach them. On 9 December, two days after the attack, 32 crew members were found alive inside the *Oklahoma*.

Luckily, the repair facilities at Pearl Harbor were not badly damaged during the attack. Salvage work began right away. Most of the sunken battleships were refloated and repaired, and the Americans were able to fix many of the cruisers and destroyers. The ships eventually returned to active service. During the salvage efforts, workers had to recover and identify the bodies of men who had died. When workers were repairing the *West Virginia*, they found chalk marks on the wall of one compartment that showed that some of the men had survived for 17 days before they died.

THE UNITED STATES DECLARES WAR

On 8 December, President Roosevelt delivered a speech to Congress, which was broadcast on the radio, describing the attack. He asked Congress to declare war on Japan. The Senate voted 82–0 in favour of war. In the House of Representatives, the vote was

"I hurried toward the side entrance of the hospital and started up the stairs to a second-floor porch. As I reached the top of the stairs — I will never forget what I saw — there were about fifteen or twenty stretchers with injured men lying on them. They were lined up head-to-toe next to the railing of the porch. There were more bloody wounds — caused by shrapnel — than I had ever seen in my life . . . .

We started operating. The air-raid sirens blew. And we heard the roar of planes over the fragile wooden hospital. We had nowhere to go. We had a patient in the middle of an operation. The big bombers, heading for Pearl Harbor, flew so low that the vibrations shook the instruments on the table . . . .

Caring for the wounded and dying went on for days. Schools were made into temporary emergency rooms. The cafeteria was used for the operating room and the kitchen was used for sterilizing instruments. There were shortages of bandages and medicines. We were not prepared for the many hundreds of casualties."

Second Lieutenant Madelyn Blonskey of the Army Nurse Corps.

Above *Japanese officials signed papers of surrender aboard the* USS Missouri *in Tokyo Bay on 2 September 1945.*

388–1, with only Representative Jeannette Rankin of Montana voting no. Three days later, Germany and Italy declared war on the United States. The US Congress responded with a resolution authorising the president to declare war on them.

THE COURSE OF THE WAR

During the next months, Japan advanced in the Pacific, taking Guam, Wake Island, and other territory. In 1942, Japan also took the Philippines. On 18 April 1942, 16 US B-25 bombers staged a daylight raid on Tokyo, Japan. The raid did little damage but slowly, things in the Pacific began to change. The turning point came in June 1942, when the Japanese suffered a major defeat at the Battle of Midway, near Hawaii. The Japanese were now on the defensive. US forces defeated Japan at Guadalcanal in 1943, took Guam in 1944, and were victorious at Iwo Jima and Okinawa in 1945.

Meanwhile, in Europe, US forces joined the British in fighting the Germans. On 6 June 1944, Allied troops landed on the French coast for the D-Day invasion. They eventually retook Paris, the Netherlands, and Belgium. By early 1945, it was clear that Germany would be defeated. Hitler killed himself on 30 April and Germany surrendered a week later.

"Yesterday, December 7th, 1941 – a date which will live in infamy – the United States of America was suddenly and deliberately attacked by naval and air forces of the Empire of Japan. The United States was at peace with that nation, and, at the solicitation of Japan, was still in conversation with its Government and its Emperor looking toward the maintenance of peace in the Pacific . . . .

The attack yesterday on the Hawaiian Islands has caused severe damage to American naval and military forces. I regret to tell you that very many American lives have been lost . . . .

[A]lways will our whole nation remember the character of the onslaught against us. No matter how long it may take us to overcome this premeditated invasion, the American people in their righteous might will win through to absolute victory . . . .

I ask that the Congress declare that since the unprovoked and dastardly attack by Japan on Sunday, December 7, a state of war has existed between the United States and the Japanese Empire."

President Franklin D. Roosevelt, asking Congress to declare war on Japan, 8 December 1941.

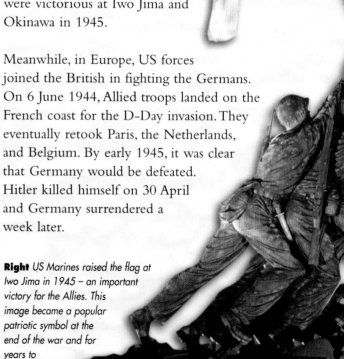

Right *US Marines raised the flag at Iwo Jima in 1945 – an important victory for the Allies. This image became a popular patriotic symbol at the end of the war and for years to come.*

Above *The atomic cloud rising over Nagasaki. Japan surrendered after the United States dropped atomic bombs on two major citites – Hiroshima and Nagasaki – in August 1945.*

But Japan kept fighting. Harry Truman – who became president after Roosevelt died on 12 April of a cerebral haemorrhage – knew that many people would die on both sides if the United States invaded Japan. Truman decided instead to use a new weapon, the atomic bomb, on Japanese cities. Nicknamed 'Little Boy', the first atomic bomb was dropped on the Japanese city of Hiroshima on 6 August, killing close to half the city's population of 300,000. President Truman warned Japan that unless it surrendered unconditionally, more of its cities would face the same fate as Hiroshima. Three days later, US bombers once again took to the skies above Japan. On 9 August, a bomb nicknamed 'Fat Man' was dropped on the city of Nagasaki instantly killing over 40,000 people. The day after the attack on Nagasaki, the emperor overruled the military and Japan surrendered on 14 August. World War II was over.

"We are in possession of the most destructive explosive ever devised by man... We have just begun to to use this weapon against your homeland. If you still have any doubt, make inquiry as to what happened to Hiroshima when just one atomic bomb fell on that city."

Extract from the leaflet dropped by the USAF on Japanese cities after 9 August 1945.

TIMELINE 1942-1945

18 APRIL 1942
United States bombs Tokyo.

4–7 JUNE 1942
United States wins Battle of Midway.

FEBRUARY 1943
United States defeats Japan at Guadalcanal.

6 JUNE 1944
D-Day invasion of France.

MARCH 1945
United States defeats Japan at Iwo Jima.

12 APRIL 1945
Roosevelt dies; Harry Truman becomes president.

30 APRIL 1945
Adolf Hitler commits suicide.

7 MAY 1945
Germany surrenders.

21 JUNE 1945
United States captures Okinawa.

Above *The Hiroshima Memorial remembers the thousands killed by the atomic bomb.*

Pearl Harbor changed the way Americans saw their place in the world. After the United States was attacked, Americans could not believe any more that an ocean would protect them from harm. The attack also made them determined to defend their country and seek revenge for the people who had been killed. On 9 December 1941, The Oregonian – a newspaper in Portland, Oregon – introduced the phrase 'Remember Pearl Harbor.' Since then, Americans have remembered Pearl Harbor in many different ways.

Above *A 1942 propaganda poster reminded Americans not to forget the attack on Pearl Harbor.*

Below *During World War II, posters with the character of Uncle Sam encouraged men to enlist in the armed forces to fight the war.*

NEWS AND SOCIETY

Americans knew that ships had been destroyed, but they did not know many details or how bad the attack was. In these days before television, many Americans got their news from newsreels, which were short films about current events shown in cinemas. A cameraman named Al Brick was in Pearl Harbor on 7 December 1941, and he shot film of the attack. The government took the film from him. A censored version was released in February 1942. This newsreel and others about Pearl Harbor served as effective propaganda. They helped keep Americans in favour of the war and against the Japanese.

Outraged by the attack on Pearl Harbor, Americans were united by strong feelings of patriotism. US Territory had never before been attacked by foreign forces. Although the United States was not attacked again during the war, Americans were ready for battle. Teenage boys and men eagerly enlisted in the armed forces. Women and girls did what they could for the war effort. With the men off fighting, many women went to work

> Down went the gunner, a bullet was his fate
> Down went the gunner, then the gunner's mate
> Up jumped the sky pilot, gave the boys a look
> And manned the gun himself as he laid aside The Book, shouting
> Praise the Lord and pass the ammunition!
> Praise the Lord and pass the ammunition!
> Praise the Lord and pass the ammunition and we'll all stay free!

🎵 **Praise the Lord and Pass the Ammunition** *by Frank Loesser, 1942.*

Above 'Remember Pearl Harbor' became a rallying cry as the United States found itself engulfed in a war it had tried to stay out of.

TIMELINE
1945-1950

6 AUGUST 1945
Atomic bomb dropped on Hiroshima.

9 AUGUST 1945
Atomic bomb dropped on Nagasaki.

14 AUGUST 1945
Japan surrenders.

2 SEPTEMBER 1945
Japan signs formal papers of surrender.

1947
Central Intelligence Agency and Joint Chiefs of Staff created.

1950
Platform with flagpole built over sunken battleship *Arizona*.

History in ev'ry century,

records an act that lives forevermore.

We'll recall, as in to line we fall

The thing that happened on Hawaii's

shore.

Let's remember Pearl Harbor

As we go to meet the foe

Let's remember Pearl Harbor

As we did the Alamo.

We will always remember

How they died for liberty.

Let's remember Pearl Harbor

And go on to victory.

🎵 **Remember Pearl Harbor by Don Reid and Sammy Kaye, 1941.**

for the first time. They found themselves acting as the heads of households and single parents. Family life was very different from what it was like before the war.

PEARL HARBOR IN SONG

The phrase 'Remember Pearl Harbor' became the title of a popular song only weeks after the attack. The lively march was written by Don Reid and the bandleader Sammy Kaye. It became one of the most popular songs of World War II. *Praise the Lord and Pass the Ammunition* was another popular song, written by the composer Frank Loesser. The song was based on the true story of a chaplain named Howell Forgy who was onboard the cruiser *New Orleans* during the attack. Forgy encouraged

Above The cover of the sheet music to Remember Pearl Harbor, a popular song from 1941.

Above Burt Lancaster starred in the 1953 film From Here to Eternity, one of many movies that used the story of Pearl Harbor as their plot.

Right Ben Affleck played a daring pilot in the action film Pearl Harbor, which was released on Memorial Day in 2001.

sailors on the ammunition line. His words to the sailors inspired the song.

THE PRINTED PAGE

Thousands of books have been published about the attack. They include both non-fiction books and novels using Pearl Harbor in the plot. One noteworthy historical book is *At Dawn We Slept: The Untold Story of Pearl Harbor* by Gordon W. Prange (1981). The book gives both the Japanese and US sides of the conflict. Many historical books trace the events leading up to the attack, while others give the eyewitness accounts of survivors. In fiction, *From Here to Eternity* by James Jones (1951) is set in Hawaii in the days before the attack. The book, which deals with the personal lives of soldiers and their families, was a best-seller. More recently, Harry Turtledove's *Days of Infamy* (2004) looked at what might have happened if the Japanese had launched a full-scale invasion of Hawaii and occupied the islands after driving the Americans out.

PEARL HARBOR ON THE SCREEN

Many films have used the dramatic story of Pearl Harbor as their plot, from the first fictional film about it – called *Remember Pearl Harbor* (1942) – to *Pearl Harbor* (2001), the big-budget special-effects film that appeared 60 years after the attack. One of the most famous films is *From Here to Eternity* (1953). Based on the book, the film won eight Academy Awards. *In Harm's Way* (1965), starring John Wayne and Kirk Douglas, also focused on the personal lives of officers who were at Pearl Harbor. *Tora! Tora! Tora!* (1970), made jointly by US and Japanese film makers, traced the road to war from both countries' sides. The film was praised for its action scenes and accuracy.

The Final Countdown (1980) was a science-fiction film about Pearl Harbor. It asked: What would happen if a modern-day nuclear aircraft carrier was somehow sent back in time to 6 December 1941? Should the crew strike against the Japanese, or should they let history take its course? The film makers got a great deal of help from the US Navy in making the film. Many viewers and critics were disappointed by *Pearl Harbor* (2001), which starred Ben Affleck and Josh Hartnett as US airmen

Above *The 1970 movie Tora! Tora! Tora! told the story of the attack from both the Japanese and American sides.*

"Pearl Harbor is about a passionate love triangle that gets interrupted when enemy planes bomb an isolated miltary outpost . . . . But it expertly capitalizes on the emotional associations Americans have with Pearl Harbor and renders the battle scenes with an excellence that goes beyond proficiency and into the realm of art."

Review of the film 'Pearl Harbor' in the San Francisco Chronicle, 25 May 2001.

caught up in romantic rivalry when the Japanese struck. The film was released on Memorial Day and had dazzling special effects. However, it contained many historical mistakes and inaccuracies and drew criticism from survivors and historians as well as poor reviews from film critics.

In spite of this, it went on to become one of the largest grossing films in US history and won an Academy Award for its sound effects.

"Here is the motion picture record released by the United States Navy of the havoc wrought by the Japs' sneak sky and sea raid on Pearl Harbor, America's mid-Pacific naval bastion. On December 7, 1941, Japan like its infamous Axis partners struck first and declared war afterwards. Costly to our Navy was the loss of war vessels, airplanes, and equipment, but more costly to Japan was the effectiveness of its foul attack in immediately unifying America in its determination to fight and win the war thrust upon it and to win the peace that will follow."

The opening lines of the newsreel The Bombing of Pearl Harbor, *released in 1942.*

Below *Pearl Harbor survivor Edmond Chappell, who served on the USS Maryland, signs an autograph during the world premiere of the film Pearl Harbor in 2001.*

LOOKING BACK PEARL HARBOR IN CONTEXT

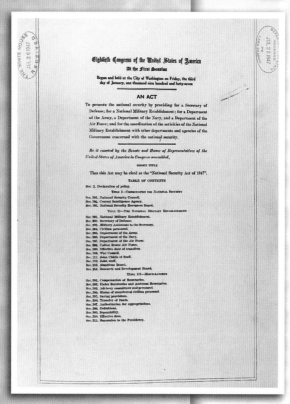

Above *President Truman signed the National Security Act on 26 July 1947.*

D ays after the attack, an official investigation began into how the United States was caught off guard by Japan. The investigation was the first of many asking the same question. In terms of the war, though, it did not really matter how Pearl Harbor happened. History has shown that the attack on Pearl Harbor did not really hurt the ability of the United States to help win the war.

WINNING THE WAR

Before Pearl Harbor, many in the US and Japanese military believed that battleships held the key to victory. World War II proved that this idea was wrong. Aircraft carriers turned out to be much more important than battleships in winning the war. At Pearl Harbor, eight US battleships were damaged, and only six could be repaired. While

"Four years ago the thoughts and fears of the whole civilized world were centered on . . . . Pearl Harbor. The mighty threat to civilization which began there is now laid at rest . . . . We shall not forget Pearl Harbor . . . . The evil done by the Japanese war lords can never be repaired or forgotten. But their power to destroy and kill has been taken from them . . . .

This is a victory of more than arms alone. This is a victory of liberty over tyranny. From our war plants rolled the tanks and planes which blasted their way to the heart of our enemies; from our shipyards sprang the ships which bridged all the oceans of the world for our weapons and supplies; from our farms came the food and fiber for our armies and navies and for our Allies in all the corners of the earth; from our mines and factories came the raw materials and the finished products which gave us the equipment to overcome our enemies. But back of it all were the will and spirit and determination of a free people — who know what freedom is, and who know that it is worth whatever price they had to pay to preserve it . . . .

As president of the United States, I proclaim Sunday, September second, 1945 to be V-J Day — the day of formal surrender by Japan . . . . It is a day which we Americans shall always remember as a day of retribution — as we remember that other day, the day of infamy."

🗨 **President Harry Truman's radio broadcast after Japan's official surrender in World War II, 2 September 1945.**

Right *A female war worker displays the freshly painted inside hatch of a submarine.*

Above *Women hard at work in a factory during World War II, producing arms and materials that helped win the war.*

TIMELINE
1951-1961

1951
Novel *From Here to Eternity* published.

1953
Film *From Here to Eternity* released.

15 MARCH 1958
President Eisenhower authorises creation of USS *Arizona* Memorial.

25 MARCH 1961
Elvis Presley gives concert to raise funds for *Arizona* Memorial.

the repair work was being done, the damaged battleships could not be used. Fortunately, the Pacific Fleet's six aircraft carriers were not damaged in the attack, and the US Navy had to depend on them. As the war went on, the carriers were very important in winning major battles for the Allies in the Pacific.

US submarines also turned out to be very important in stopping the Imperial Japanese Navy. The Japanese had not bombed the US submarine base at Pearl Harbor, which was a big mistake for the Japanese. In addition, while the Japanese destroyed many American planes, they were older aircraft that were soon replaced by new, more modern planes. In fact, US shipyards and factories were able to produce new ships

They started somethin'
But we're gonna end it
Right in their own back yard!
We're proud of our country
And proud to defend it
So, Yankee Doodle, hit 'em hard!
Put our shoulders to the wheel
The whole darn world will get a brand new deal!
Oh! They started somethin'
But we're gonna end it
Right in their own back yard!

They Started Somethin' (But We're Gonna End It!) by Robert Sour, Don McCrea, and Ernest Gold, performed by Kate Smith, recorded 16 December 1941. The song showed how committed Americans were to do what was necessary to win the war.

Above *Everyone did his or her part to help the Allies win the war.*

"The Japanese attack was a complete surprise to the commanders and they failed to make suitable dispositions to meet such an attack. Each failed properly to evaluate the seriousness of the situation. These errors of judgment were the effective causes for the success of the attack."

Excerpt from the report of the Roberts Commission, 23 January 1942, blaming Admiral Kimmel and General Short for the attack on Pearl Harbor.

and planes very quickly to replace those that were damaged or destroyed at Pearl Harbor. The Japanese were not able to produce large numbers of new weapons quickly like the Americans.

The Japanese made another big mistake at Pearl Harbor. They did not attack the US oil tanks and maintenance facilities. This meant that the United States still had a large supply of valuable oil. The United States could also repair and build ships and planes right at Pearl Harbor instead of on the West Coast, which was farther away from where the war was being fought in the Pacific. The Japanese also did not attack an administration building at Pearl Harbor that contained a code-breaking intelligence unit. The unit provided significant information that helped the United States win the Battle of Midway in 1942.

Above *The USS* Arizona *Memorial at Pearl Harbor is a permanent reminder of the many lives lost when the battleship sank during the attack.*

OFFICIAL INVESTIGATIONS

Admiral Kimmel and General Short were relieved of their commands and had their ranks lowered shortly after Pearl Harbor. President Roosevelt appointed a commission to find out if the attack could have been prevented. The official commission, headed by Supreme Court Justice Owen Roberts, made its report in January 1942. The report said that Kimmel and Short were "solely responsible" for Japan's success in the attack. The report accused them of "dereliction of duty" for not making reasonable preparations to defend Pearl Harbor. Kimmel and Short both retired in 1942. Kimmel protested for the rest of

"The reasons for the disastrous defeat at Pearl Harbor form a tapestry woven of many threads, including the inevitable advantage of an aggressor free to choose the time, place, and form of a surprise attack in a time of nominal peace, and the brilliant planning and flawless execution by a Japanese Navy whose capabilities were seriously underestimated by many Americans . . . . The attack on Pearl Harbor probably could not have been prevented . . . .

It is clear today ... that Admiral Kimmel and General Short were not solely responsible for the defeat at Pearl Harbor. To say that Admiral Kimmel and General Short were not solely responsible does not, however, necessarily imply that they were totally blameless . . . .

Advocates for Admiral Kimmel and General Short argue, in effect, that the failure of Washington officials to provide the critical intercepts to the Hawaiian commanders excuses any errors made in Hawaii. It does not. No warfighting commander ever has enough information or enough resources. It is the job of the commander to carry out his or her mission as best he or she can with the information and resources available to him or her."

 Excerpt from the Department of Defense report on the attack on Pearl Harbor, 1995.

Right *Members of President Roosevelt's committee investigating the attacks on Pearl Harbor.*

his life that he was not given the key information he needed that would have let him prepare for the attack.

Ten official investigations looked into the attack over the years. Congress set up a committee that held hearings in 1945 and 1946, after World War II ended. As a result of this investigation, the Central Intelligence Agency was created in 1947 to collect and analyse intelligence information. The Joint Chiefs of Staff was created the same year to improve coordination and communication between the Army and Navy.

Above The seal of the Central Intelligence Agency (CIA). The CIA was created by the National Security Act of 26 July 1947.

In 1995, the US Department of Defense released a report stating that many people – both civilians and military personnel – shared the blame for the United States not being prepared for the attack. The report stated that officials in Washington, D.C., did not tell Kimmel and Short important things about Japan. Kimmel and Short, however, had not realised that their most important responsibility was preparing for war with Japan. The most serious overall mistake, according to the report, was Washington's delay in delivering the final warning to Hawaii on 7 December. In May 1999, the Senate voted to recommend that Kimmel and Short be cleared of all charges against them. No action was taken on this recommendation.

After the terrorist attacks on the World Trade Center and the Pentagon on 11 September 2001, many Americans looked back at Pearl Harbor.

Above Fans cluster around Elvis Presley in Los Angeles on his way to Hawaii to film *Blue Hawaii*. While there, Presley also performed at the benefit concert for Pearl Harbor.

Above USS Missouri Memorial at Pearl Harbor.

In both 1941 and 2001, the United States had intelligence information, but no one acted on it. "In Pearl Harbor there is not much doubt that the US had received enough intelligence to predict the event, but failed to predict it," said historian Alan Brinkley of Columbia University. "Historians of intelligence argue that it doesn't matter how much information you have if you are not looking for what it tells you." US officials in 1941 simply could not imagine that the Japanese would stage such a risky attack so far from home.

Over the years, some people have claimed that there was a conspiracy involving Pearl Harbor. They think that Roosevelt and others knew about the attack ahead of time but did nothing because they wanted the United States to enter the war. There has been no solid evidence to support this idea.

PEARL HARBOR TODAY

Pearl Harbor is now officially called the Navy Region Hawaii and is still an important military installation. It is the headquarters of five major fleet commands, including the Pacific Fleet. More than 80,000 people live and work there, including members of the armed forces, their families, and civilian employees. Pearl Harbor is also the site of the USS *Arizona* Memorial. The battleship *Arizona* was never raised from the sea, and the bodies of the 1,177 sailors who died there were never recovered.

In 1950, the commander of the Pacific Fleet had a wooden platform

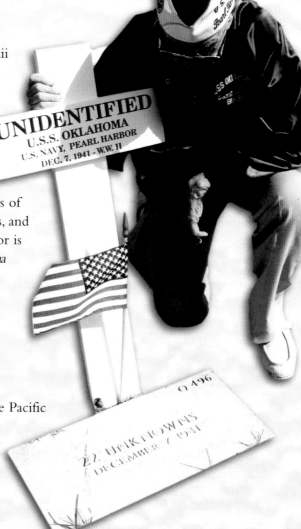

Right Veteran Paul Goody remembers the unidentified dead of the Pearl Harbor attack.

On March 7, 1950, the US flag was raised over the wreck of the USS *Arizona*. The following statements were made at the ceremony:

"We are here this morning to do honor to the USS *Arizona* and her splendid crew, so many of whom are still with the ship. From today on the *Arizona* will again fly our country's flag just as proudly as she did on the morning of December 7, 1941. I am sure the *Arizona* crew will know and appreciate what we are doing."

Admiral Arthur W. Radford, commander in chief of the Pacific Fleet.

"May our efforts now be viewed as a solemn covenant to our fallen comrades, a covenant to complete the tasks which will help shape a better world for tomorrow. Grant that flag we are about to raise will ever stand as a symbol to our devotion to those virtues which have made our nation great."

Captain E. B. Harp, chaplain of the Pacific Fleet.

PICTURE CREDITS:

Every effort has been made to trace the copyright holders, and we apologise in advance for any unintentional ommisions. We would be pleased to insert the appropriate acknowledgements in any subsequent edition of this publication.

B=bottom; C=centre; L=left; R=right; T=top

20th Century Fox/Everett/Rex Features: 7t, 33t. AP/AP/PA Photos: 36-37. Courtesy of Michael Barnes: 31b. Bettmann/Corbis: OFCb, 5b, 11r, 12t, 15b, 18t, 18-19, 19cr, 20-21, 24t, 24b, 26c, 26-27, 28t, 33b, 37br, 40tl, 40tr, 41tl, 41tr, 41b, 43tr. British Museum, London, UK/The Bridgeman Art Library: 8t. Central Intelligence Agency: 37t. Check Six/ Getty Images: 2. Corbis: 7b, 10bl, 11c, 16-17, 19t, 30b, 35b, 42tl, 42tr, 43tl, 43b. CSU Archives/Everett Collection/Rex Features: 15t, 17cr, 31t, 42b. David J. & Janice L. Frent Collection/Corbis: 5t. Everett Collection/Rex Features: 32t, 32b. Getty Images: 17t, 38b. Hulton Archive/Getty Images: 26t. Hulton-Deutsch Collection/Corbis: OFCtl, OBC (background), Douglas Kirkland/Corbis: OFCt (background). iStock: OBCbl, br. Minnesota Historical Society/Corbis: 14t. Vito Palmisano/Getty Images: 28-29. National Archives and Records Administration: 21t, 21r, 25, 29t, 34t. Courtesy of the National Security Agency: 20t. Naval Historical Center Online Library: 40b. Douglas Peebles/Stock Connection/Rex Features: 1, 39b. Photo Resource Hawaii/Alamy: 10-11. The Print Collector/Alamy: 8br. Private Collection/Archives Charmet/The Bridgeman Art Library: 9b. Rex Features: 12-13. Martin Sanders/www.mapart.co.uk: 16t. Shutterstock: OBCtl, tr, 4-5 (background), 6-7 (background), 29b, 36t, 38t, 39t, 48. Sipa Press/Rex Features: 4b. Tavin/Everett/Rex Features: 14b. Hayley Terry: 22t. Underwood & Underwood/Corbis: 13br. Witold Skrypczak/Alamy: 23. Swim Ink 2, LLC/Corbis: 6t. ticktock Media Archive: 4t. Time & Life Pictures/Getty Images: 6b, 27t, 34b. United States Office of War Information/Wikimedia Commons 30t. Roger-Viollet/Rex Features: 12b, 22b, 35t.